RENAL DIET COOKBOOK

ULTIMATE GUIDE FOR BEGINNERS TO LOW SODIUM, LOW POTASSIUM, LOW PHOSPHORUS, HEALTHY KIDNEY RECIPES & 4 WEEK MEAL PLAN TO IMPROVE KIDNEY FUNCTION

CAROLINE MCGUIRE

Contents

Introduction

Renal Diet

A renal diet is a specific type of diet that can help control or prevent kidney disease. These diets may recommend limiting your intake of foods with added salt, potassium, and protein. Non-renal diets are also available and may include low-sodium or low cholesterol and other diets appropriate to a person's medical needs. A renal diet may treat people with various conditions, such as heart disease, diabetes, or obesity. Other lifestyle changes that may benefit people with kidney disease include restrictions on caffeine, alcohol, and a low-oxalate diet. Other renal diets include partial fasting or semi-fasting, where the person fasts part of the day while eating different foods in typical amounts. This type of diet either partial fasting or semi-fasting refeeding syndrome. The kidneys help control the body's functions. The kidneys can produce urine that is neither too dilute (dehydrated) nor too concentrated (hypertonic). Too much or too little fluid in the blood may cause electrolyte imbalances and health problems. The kidneys are also complex in regulating blood pressure, maintaining acid-base homeostasis, and producing hormones that play a role in blood clotting, red blood cell production, and regulation of muscle tone. Nutrition is a fundamental part of treating people with chronic kidney disease. One of the most significant dietary changes a person with kidney disease must make is to limit sodium in their diet. Excess sodium in the body can result in fluid retention, putting extra pressure on the kidneys.

When starting a renal diet or restricting your sodium intake, it's essential to consult your doctor or a registered dietitian because renal diets may need to be tailored to meet your specific needs. A dietitian can also help you plan menus and meal options that fit your tastes and budget.

To avoid consuming too much sodium, you can save food with added salt. Salt is usually found in processed and fast foods, such as chips, canned vegetables, and soups. It may also be added to most table meats, canned vegetables, and potato products. Some people can safely eat small amounts of salted fish in moderation. Eating salt-cured fish such as salmon or tuna is an excellent way to get enough sodium if you don't like the taste of salty meats or fish.

If you have kidney failure, your doctor or dietitian may recommend a deficient diet in potassium. The potassium levels in all foods are significant to people with kidney disease. Potassium is a mineral that comes from the soil and is found in red meat, poultry, salmon, milk, bananas, and avocados. Because kidney disease can affect the filtering process of your kidneys, it's essential to be careful with your potassium intake.

This renal diet cookbook includes recipes with low potassium levels. Foods and recipes that are naturally high in potassium are also included, to still eat a healthy, broad diet that consists of all of the nutrients your body needs.

The main focus of this cookbook is low in potassium while still allowing you to eat a wide variety of healthy foods. Recipes include healthy foods such as lean meats, whole grains, and vegetables. Even though this is primarily a low potassium diet, it's also a healthy diet that includes nutrient-rich foods.

FIVE STAGES OF CHRONIC KIDNEY DISEASE

STAGES	DESCRIPTION
Stage 1	Few or no symptoms
Stage 2	Mild reduction of kidney function and some symptoms
Stage 3	Moderate reduction of kidney function and more symptoms (but not needing dialysis)
Stage 4	Severe reduction of kidney function and requiring either hemodialysis or peritoneal dialysis
Stage 5	Kidney failure that requires transplantation.

Stages 1-3 are asymptomatic stages. If the decrease in kidney function is mild, few or no symptoms may be experienced, and the diagnosis of CKD may only be discovered by screening. Stages 4-5 are symptomatic stages. Many people with CKD experience reduced kidney function and develop anemia, fatigue, and weight loss as they age. Others may experience muscle pain (sarcopenia) or bone pain (osteoporosis).

RECOMMENDED AND NOT RECOMMENDED FOODS

NOT RECOMMENDED FOODS	RECOMMENDED FOODS
Canned Foods	Pineapples
Potatoes and sweet potatoes	Whole-Wheat Bread
Processed Meats	Oranges and Orange Juice
Instant Foods	Eggs
Sugar and processed foods	Red meats
Dairy products	Fish
Beans	Bananas

Breakfast

SAUSAGE CHEESE BAKE OMELETTE

10
Minutes

45
Minutes

8

Ingredients

- 16 eggs
- 2 cups Cheddar cheese, shredded
- 1/2 cup salsa
- 1 lb. ground sausage
- 1 1/2 cups coconut milk
- Pepper
- Salt

Directions

1. Preheat the oven to 350°F.
2. Add sausage to a pan and cook until browned. Drain excess fat.
3. In a large bowl, whisk eggs and milk. Stir in cheese, cooked sausage, and salsa.
4. Pour the omelet mixture into the baking dish and bake for 45 minutes.
5. Serve and enjoy.

Nutrition

Calories 360; Fat 24g; Carbohydrates: 4g; Sugar: 3g; Protein: 28g; Cholesterol: 400mg; Phosphorus: 165mg; Potassium: 370mg; Sodium: 135mg.

BLUEBERRY MUFFINS

15
Minutes

30
Minutes

12

Ingredients

- 2 cups unsweetened rice milk
- 1 tbsp. apple cider vinegar
- 3 ½ cups all-purpose flour
- 1 cup granulated sugar
- 1 tbsp. baking soda substitute
- 1 tsp. ground cinnamon
- ½ tsp. ground nutmeg
- A pinch ground ginger
- ½ cup canola oil
- 2 tbsp. pure vanilla extract
- 2 ½ cups fresh blueberries

Directions

1. Preheat the oven to 375°F.
2. Prepare a muffin pan and set it aside.
3. Stir together the rice milk and vinegar in a small bowl. Set aside for 10 minutes.
4. In a large bowl, stir together the sugar, flour, baking soda, cinnamon, nutmeg, and ginger until well mixed.
5. Add oil and vanilla to the milk and mix.
6. Put milk mixture to dry ingredients and stir well to combine.
7. Put the blueberries and spoon the muffin batter evenly into the cups.
8. Bake the muffins for 25 to 30 minutes or until golden, and a toothpick comes out clean.
9. Cool for 15 minutes and serve.

Nutrition

Calories: 331; Fat: 11g Carb: 52g; Protein: 6g; Sodium: 35mg; Potassium: 89mg; Phosphorus: 90mg.

COCONUT BREAKFAST SMOOTHIE

| 5 Minutes | 5 Minutes | 1 |

Ingredients

- 1/4 cup whey protein powder
- 1/2 cup coconut milk
- 5 drops liquid stevia
- 1 tbsp. coconut oil
- 1 tsp. vanilla
- 2 tbsp. coconut butter
- 1/4 cup water
- 1/2 cup ice

Directions

1. Add all the ingredients into the blender and blend until smooth.
2. Serve and enjoy

Nutrition

Calories 560; Fat 45g; Carbohydrates: 12g; Sugar: 4g; Protein: 25g; Cholesterol: 60mg; Phosphorus: 160mg; Potassium: 127mg; Sodium: 85mg.

GRANDMA'S PANCAKE SPECIAL

5
Minutes

15
Minutes

3

Ingredients

- 1 tbsp. oil
- 1 cup almond milk
- 1 egg
- 2 tsp. sodium-free baking powder
- 2 tbsp. sugar
- 1 ¼ cups flour

Directions

1. Mix all the dry ingredients such as flour, sugar, and baking powder.
2. Combine oil, almond milk, and egg in another bowl. Once done, add them all to the flour mixture.
3. Make sure that as your stir the mixture, blend them until slightly lumpy.
4. In a hot, greased skillet, pour in at least ¼ cup of the batter to make each pancake.
5. Ensure that the bottom is a bit brown, then turn and cook the other side.

Nutrition

Calories: 167; Carbs: 50g; Protein: 11g; Fats: 11g; Phosphorus: 176mg; Potassium: 215mg; Sodium: 70mg.

FRENCH TOAST WITH APPLESAUCE

5
Minutes

15
Minutes

6

Ingredients

- ¼ cup unsweetened applesauce
- ½ cup almond milk
- 1 tsp. ground cinnamon
- 2 eggs
- 2 tbsp. white sugar

Directions

1. Mix well applesauce, sugar, cinnamon, almond milk, and eggs in a mixing bowl.
2. Soak the bread, one by one, into the applesauce mixture until wet.
3. On medium fire, heat a nonstick skillet greased with cooking spray.
4. Add soaked bread one at a time and cook for 2–3 minutes per side or until lightly browned.
5. Serve and enjoy.

Nutrition

Calories: 57; Carbs: 6g; Protein: 4g; Fats: 4g; Phosphorus: 69mg; Potassium: 88mg; Sodium: 43mg.

WAFFLES

| 20 Minutes | 15 Minutes | 8 |

Ingredients

- 1 and ½ tsp. yeast for baking
- 8 tbsp. butter, unsalted
- 2 eggs
- 1 and ¾ cups milk—2% milkfat
- Sugar substitute to taste
- 1 tsp. almond extract
- 2 cups flour—all-purpose

Directions

1. Heat a saucepan and place the butter and milk in it. Wait for the butter to melt with occasional stirring. As you are waiting for the milk and butter mixture to cool off a bit so that the saucepan is warm to the touch, you will take a bowl and whisk sugar substitute, yeast, and flour. Once combined, you will add the warm milk and butter mixture to the flour bowl and whisk some more until the mass is well combined.
2. Take another bowl and whisk the eggs with almond extract, adding the flour batter's whipped egg mixture. Stir well to combine until you get a smooth, homogenous mass. The best option is to prepare the mixture a day ahead, as you will need to keep the dough in the fridge for at least 12 hours before baking.
3. Once you are ready to bake your waffles, you will set the oven to 200°F and keep the waffle bowl near to keep the dough warm. Prepare your waffle maker and start making waffles by pouring the dough.

Nutrition

Potassium: 131 mg; Sodium: 208 mg; Phosphorus: 113 mg; Calories: 223.

Lunch

BEEF STIR-FRY

5
Minutes

15
Minutes

4

Ingredients

- 4 cups water
- 2 tbsp. cornstarch
- 2 tsp. honey
- 6 tbsp. Worcestershire sauce
- 1 tbsp. minced fresh ginger
- 1-pound boneless beef round steak, cut into thin strips
- 1 tbsp. olive oil
- 3 cups broccoli florets
- 2 carrots, thinly sliced
- 1 (6 ounces) package frozen pea pods, thawed
- 2 tbsp. chopped onion
- 1 (8 ounces) can sliced water chestnuts, untrained
- 1 cup cabbage
- ½ cup kale, chopped
- 1 tbsp. olive oil

Directions

1. Combine corn starch, honey, and Worcestershire sauce, in a small bowl until smooth. Stir in ginger; toss the beef in sauce to coat.
2. Heat 1 tbsp. oil in a large skillet over medium-high heat. Cook and stir broccoli, carrots, pea pods, and onion for 1 minute. Stir in water chestnuts, cabbage, and kale; cover and simmer until vegetables are tender, about 4 minutes. Remove from skillet and keep warm.
3. In the same skillet, heat 1 tbsp. oil over medium-high heat. Cook and stir beef until the desired degree of doneness, about 2 minutes per side for medium. Return vegetables to skillet; cook and stir until heated through about 3 minutes.

Nutrition

Calories: 139; Total Fat: 3.9g; Saturated Fat: 0.8g; Cholesterol: 12mg; Sodium: 972mg; Total Carbohydrate: 18.7g; Dietary Fiber: 4g; Total Sugar: 5.8g.

VEGETABLE CASSEROLE

| 15 Minutes | 15 Minutes | 8 |

Ingredients

- 1 tsp. olive oil
- 1 sweet onion, chopped
- 1 tsp. garlic, minced
- 2 zucchinis, chopped
- 1 red bell pepper, diced
- 2 carrots, chopped
- 2 cups low-sodium vegetable stock
- 2 large Red bell peppers, chopped
- 2 cups broccoli florets
- 1 tsp. ground coriander
- ½ tsp. ground comminutes
- Black pepper

Directions

1. Heat the olive oil in a big pan over medium-high heat.
2. Add onion and garlic. Softly cook for about 3 minutes until softened.
3. Include the zucchini, carrots, bell pepper, and softly cook for 5–6 minutes.
4. Pour the vegetable stock, Red bell peppers, broccoli, coriander, cumin, and pepper, and stir well.
5. Softly cook for about 5 minutes over medium-high heat until the vegetables are tender.
6. Serve hot and enjoy!

Nutrition

Calories: 47; Fat: 1g; Cholesterol: 0g; Carbohydrates: 8g; Sugar: 6g; Fiber: 2g; Protein: 2g; Sodium: 104mg; Calcium: 36mg; Phosphorus: 52mg; Potassium: 298 mg.

APPETIZING RICE SALAD

| 20 Minutes | 60 Minutes | 8 |

Ingredients

- 1 cup wild rice
- 2 cups water
- 1 tbsp. olive oil
- 2/3 cup walnuts, chopped
- 1 (4 inches) celery rib, sliced
- 4 scallions, thinly sliced
- 1 medium red apple, cored and diced
- ½ cup pomegranate seeds
- ½ tbsp. lemon zest
- 3 tbsp. lemon juice
- Black pepper
- 1/3 cup olive oil

Directions

1. The wild strained rice together with water and olive oil in a big pot place.
2. Bring to a boil and simmer for about 50 minutes until rice is tender.
3. In a mixing bowl, add celery, walnuts, apple, scallions, pomegranate seeds, and lemon zest.
4. Mix the lemon juice, pepper, and olive oil well with a blender.
5. Spread half of this dressing on the apple mixture and mix well.
6. When the rice is cooked, let it cool and incorporate it with the fruit mixture
7. Season with the remaining dressing.
8. Serve at room temperature and enjoy!

Nutrition

Calories: 300; Fat 19g; Cholesterol: 0mg; Carbohydrates: 34g; Sugar: 11g; Fiber: 5g; Protein: 6g; Sodium: 6mg; Calcium: 30mg; Phosphorus: 144mg; Potassium: 296 mg.

EASY LETTUCE WRAPS

15
Minutes

0
Minutes

4

Ingredients

- 8 ounces cooked chicken, shredded
- 1 scallion, chopped
- ½ cup seedless red grapes, halved
- 1 celery stalk, chopped
- ¼ cup mayonnaise
- A pinch ground black pepper
- 4 large lettuce leaves

Directions

1. Add the scallion, chicken, celery, grapes, and mayonnaise to a mixing bowl.
2. Stir well until incorporated.
3. Season with pepper.
4. Place the lettuce leaves onto serving plates.
5. Place the chicken salad onto the leaves.
6. Serve and enjoy!

Nutrition

Calories: 146; Fat: 5g; Cholesterol: 35mg; Carbohydrates: 8g; Sugar: 4g; Fiber: 0g; Protein: 16g; Sodium: 58mg; Calcium: 18mg; Phosphorus: 125mg; Potassium: 212 mg.

CRISPY LEMON CHICKEN

| 10 Minutes | 10 Minutes | 6 |

Ingredients

- 1 lb. boneless and skinless chicken breast
- ½ cup all-purpose flour
- 1 large egg
- ½ cup lemon juice
- 2 tbsp. water
- ¼ tsp. salt
- ¼ tsp. lemon pepper
- 1 tsp. mixed herb seasoning
- 2 tbsp. olive oil
- A few lemon slices for garnishing
- 1 tbsp. chopped parsley (for garnishing)
- 2 cups cooked plain white rice

Directions

1. Slice the chicken breast thin and season with herbs, salt, and pepper.
2. In a small bowl, whisk together the egg with the water.
3. Keep the flour in a separate bowl.
4. Dip the chicken slices in the egg bath and then into the flour.
5. Heat your oil in a medium frying pan.
6. Shallow fry the chicken in the pan until golden brown.
7. Add the lemon juice and cook for another couple of minutes.
8. Take the chicken out of the pan and transfer it to a wide dish with absorbing paper to absorb any excess oil.
9. Garnish with some chopped parsley and lemon wedges on top.
10. Serve with rice.

Nutrition

Calories: 232; Carbohydrate: 24g; Protein: 18g; Fat: 8g; Sodium: 100g; Potassium: 234mg; Phosphorus: 217mg.

MEXICAN CHORIZO SAUSAGE

10
Minutes

15
Minutes

1

Ingredients

- 2 pounds boneless pork but coarsely ground
- 3 tbsp. red wine vinegar
- 2 tbsp. smoked paprika
- ½ tsp. cinnamon
- ½ tsp. ground cloves
- ¼ tsp. coriander seeds
- ¼ tsp. ground ginger
- 1 tsp. ground cumin
- 3 tbsp. brandy

Directions

1. In a large mixing bowl, combine the ground pork with the seasonings, brandy, and vinegar and mix with your hands well.
2. Place the mixture into a large Ziplock bag and leave it in the fridge overnight.
3. Form into 15–16 patties of equal size.
4. Heat the oil in a large pan and fry the patties for 5–7 minutes on each side, or until the meat inside is no longer pink, and there is a light brown crust on top.
5. Serve hot.

Nutrition

Calories: 134; Carbohydrate: 0 g; Protein: 10 g; Fat: 7 g; Sodium: 40 mg; Potassium: 138 mg; Phosphorus: 128 mg.

Dinner

SPICY CABBAGE DISH

10
Minutes

240
Minutes

4

Ingredients

- 2 yellow onions, chopped
- 10 cups red cabbage, shredded
- 1 cup plums, pitted and chopped
- 1 tsp. cinnamon powder
- 1 garlic clove, minced
- 1 tsp. cumin seeds
- ¼ tsp. cloves, ground
- 2 tbsp. red wine vinegar
- 1 tsp. coriander seeds - ½ cup water

Directions

1. Add cabbage, onion, plums, garlic, cumin, cinnamon, cloves, vinegar, coriander, and water to your Slow Cooker. Stir well. Place lid and cook on LOW for 4 hours. Divide between serving platters.
2. Enjoy!

Nutrition

Calories: 197; Fat: 1g; Carbohydrates: 14g; Protein: 3g; Phosphorus: 115mg;
Potassium: 119mg; Sodium: 75mg.

BEEF ENCHILADAS

| 10 Minutes | 30 Minutes | 1 |

Ingredients

- 1-pound lean beef
- 12 whole-wheat tortillas
- 1 can low-sodium enchilada sauce
- ½ cup onion (diced)
- ½ tsp. black pepper
- 1 garlic clove
- 1 tbsp. olive oil
- 1 tsp. cumin

Directions

1. Heat the oven to 375°F
2. In a medium-sized frying pan, cook the beef in olive oil until completely cooked.
3. Add the minced garlic, diced onion, cumin, and black pepper to the pan and mix everything with the beef.
4. In a separate pan, cook the tortillas in olive oil and dip each cooked tortilla in the enchilada sauce.
5. Fill the tortilla with the meat mixture and roll it up.
6. Put the finished product in a slightly heated pan with cheese on top.
7. Bake the tortillas in the pan until crispy, golden brown, and the cheese is melted.

Nutrition

Calories: 177; Fat: 6g; Carbs: 15g; Protein: 15g; Sodium: 501mg; Potassium: 231mg; Phosphorus: 98mg.

CALIFORNIA PORK CHOPS

10 Minutes

10 Minutes

2

Ingredients

- 1 tbsp. fresh cilantro, chopped
- 1/2 cup chives, chopped
- 2 large green bell peppers, chopped
- 1 lb. 1" thick boneless pork chops
- 1 tbsp. fresh lime juice
- 2 cups cooked rice
- 1/8 tsp. dried oregano leaves
- 1/4 tsp. ground black pepper
- 1/4 tsp. ground cumin
- 1 tbsp. butter
- 1 lime

Directions

1. Start by seasoning the pork chops with lime juice and cilantro.
2. Place them in a shallow dish.
3. Toss the chives with pepper, cumin, butter, oregano, and rice in a bowl.
4. Stuff the bell peppers with this mixture and place them around the pork chops.
5. Cover the chop and bell peppers with a foil sheet and bake them for 10 minutes in the oven at 375°F.
6. Serve warm.

Nutrition

Calories: 265 kcal; Total Fat: 15g; Saturated Fat: 0g; Cholesterol: 86mg; Sodium: 70mg; Total Carbs: 24g; Fiber: 1g; Sugar: 0g; Protein: 34g.

SEAFOOD CASSEROLE

| 20 Minutes | 45 Minutes | 1 |

Ingredients

- 2 cups, peeled and diced into 1-inch pieces of eggplant
- butter, for greasing the baking dish
- 1 tbsp. olive oil
- ½ chopped sweet onion
- 1 tsp. minced garlic
- 1 chopped celery stalk
- ½ boiled and chopped red bell pepper
- 3 tbsps. freshly squeezed lemon juice
- 1 tsp. hot sauce
- ¼ tsp. creole seasoning mix
- ½ cup uncooked white rice
- 1 large egg
- 4 oz. cooked shrimp
- 6 oz. queen crab meat

Directions

1. Preheat the oven to 350°F.
2. Boil the eggplant in a saucepan for 5 minutes. Drain and set aside.
3. Grease a 9-by-13-inch baking dish with butter and set aside.
4. Heat the olive oil in a large skillet over medium heat.
5. Sauté the garlic, onion, celery, and bell pepper for 4 minutes or until tender.
6. Add the sautéed vegetables to the eggplant, lemon juice, hot sauce, seasoning, rice, and egg.
7. Stir to combine.
8. Fold in the shrimp and crab meat.
9. Spoon the casserole mixture into the casserole dish, patting down the top.
10. Bake for 25 to 30 minutes or until casserole is heated through and rice is tender. Serve warm.

Nutrition

Calories: 118; Fat: 4g; Carb: 9g; Protein: 12g; Sodium: 235mg; Potassium: 199mg; Phosphorus: 102mg.

CHICKEN AND BROCCOLI CASSEROLE

15
Minutes

45/60
Minutes

1

Ingredients

- 2 cups rice (cooked)
- 3 chicken breasts
- 2 cups broccoli
- 1 onion (diced)
- 2 eggs
- 2 cups cheddar cheese
- 2 tbsp. butter
- 1–2 tbsp. parmesan cheese

Directions

1. Heat the oven to 350°F
2. Add the broccoli to a bowl and cover it with plastic wrap. Microwave the broccoli for 2–3 minutes.
3. Dice the onion and add it with the chicken and the butter into the pan.
4. Cook the chicken for 15 minutes.
5. Once the chicken is cooked, mix it, broccoli, and rice together, and add to a greased casserole dish.
6. Add the grated cheese into the casserole dish and stir well.
7. Add the parmesan cheese on top.
8. Place the casserole dish in the oven for 30–45 minutes.

Nutrition

Calories: 349; Fat: 12g; Carbs: 14g; Protein: 44g; Sodium: 980mg; Potassium: 713mg; Phosphorus: 451mg.

Main Dishes

BAKED FRENCH TOAST CASSEROLE

20
Minutes

45
Minutes

12

Ingredients

- 1 lb. French bread
- 1 cup egg white liquid
- 6 eggs
- 1/3 cup maple syrup
- 1-1/2 cups rice almond milk,
- ½ lb. raspberries
- ½ lb. blueberries
- 1 tsp. vanilla extract
- ¾ cup strawberries

Directions

1. Slice the bread into small cubes. Keep them in a greased casserole dish.
2. Add all the berries. Only leave a few for the topping.
3. Whisk together the egg whites, eggs, rice almond milk, and maple syrup in a bowl.
4. Combine well.
5. Put the egg mixture on top of the bread. Press the bread down. All pieces should be soaked well.
6. Add berries on the top. Fill up the holes, if any.
7. Refrigerate covered for a couple of hours at least.
8. Take out the casserole half an hour before baking.
9. Set your oven to 350°F.
10. Now, bake your casserole uncovered for 30 minutes.
11. Bake for another 15 minutes, covered with a foil.
12. Let it rest for 15 minutes.
13. Serve it warm with maple syrup.

Nutrition

Calories: 200; Carbohydrates: 31g; Cholesterol: 93mg; Total Fat: 4g; Protein: 10g; Fiber: 2g; Sodium: 288mg; Sugar: 10g.

CRANBERRY DIP WITH FRESH FRUIT

10
Minutes

0
Minutes

8

Ingredients

- 8-ounce sour cream
- 1/2 cup whole berry cranberry sauce
- 1/4 tsp. nutmeg
- 1/4 tsp. ground ginger
- 4 cups fresh pineapple, peeled, cubed
- 4 medium apples, peeled, cored, and cubed
- 4 medium pears, peeled, cored, and cubed
- 1 tsp. lemon juice

Directions

1. Start by adding cranberry sauce, sour cream, ginger, and nutmeg to a food processor.
2. Blend the mixture until it's smooth, then transfer it to a bowl.
3. Toss the pineapple with pears, apples, and lemon juice in a salad bowl.
4. Thread the fruits onto mini skewers.
5. Serve them with the sauce.

Nutrition

calories: 70; Protein: 0g; Carbohydrates: 13g; Fat: 2g; Cholesterol: 4mg; Sodium: 8mg; Potassium: 101mg; Phosphorus: 15mg; Calcium: 17mg; Fiber: 1.5g.

CUCUMBERS WITH SOUR CREAM

| 10 Minutes | 0 Minutes | 4 |

Ingredients

- 2 medium cucumbers, peeled and sliced thinly
- 1/2 medium sweet onion, sliced
- 1/4 cup white wine vinegar
- 1 tbsp. Canola oil
- 1/8 tsp. black pepper
- 1/2 cup reduced-fat sour cream

Directions

1. Toss in cucumber, onion, and other ingredients in a medium-sized bowl.
2. Mix well and refrigerate for 2 hours.
3. Toss again and serve to enjoy.

Nutrition

calories: 64; Protein: 1g; Carbohydrates: 4g; Fat: 5g; Cholesterol: 3mg; Sodium: 72mg; Potassium: 113mg; Phosphorus: 24mg; Calcium: 21mg; Fiber: 0.8g.

SWEET, SAVORY MEATBALLS

10
Minutes

20
Minutes

12

Ingredients

- 1-pound ground turkey
- 1 large egg
- 1/4 cup bread crumbs
- 2 tbsp. onion, finely chopped
- 1 tsp. garlic powder
- 1/2 tsp. black pepper
- 1/4 cup canola oil
- 6-ounce grape jelly
- 1/4 cup chili sauce

Directions

1. Place all ingredients except chili sauce and jelly in a large mixing bowl.
2. Mix well until evenly mixed, then make small balls out of this mixture.
3. It will make about 48 meatballs. Spread them out on a greased pan on a stovetop.
4. Cook them over medium heat until brown on all the sides.
5. Mix chili sauce with jelly in a microwave-safe bowl and heat it for 2 minutes in the microwave.
6. Pour this chili sauce mixture onto the meatballs in the pan.
7. Transfer the meatballs to the pan to the preheated oven.
8. Bake the meatballs for 20 minutes in an oven at 375°F.
9. Serve fresh and warm.

Nutrition

calories: 127; Protein: 9g; Carbohydrates: 14g; Fat: 4g; Cholesterol: 41mg; Sodium: 129mg; Potassium: 148mg; Phosphorus: 89mg; Calcium: 15mg; Fiber: 0.2g.

Snacks

THAI TURKEY STIR FRY

| 5 Minutes | 15 Minutes | 6 |

Ingredients

- 1 1/2 lb. lean ground turkey
- 1-2 cups Thai basil, chopped
- 1 onion, cut in slivers
- 1 red bell pepper, cut in thin strips
- 2 tbsp. fresh lime juice
- What you'll need from the store cupboard:
- 2-3 large garlic cloves, peeled and sliced
- 1 tbsp. + 1 tsp. peanut oil
- 1 tbsp. fish sauce
- 1 tbsp. sriracha sauce
- 1 tbsp. soy sauce
- 1 tbsp. honey

Directions

1. In a small bowl, whisk together lime juice, fish sauce, sriracha, soy sauce, and honey.
2. Place a large wok or heavy skillet over high heat. Once the pan gets hot, add 1 tbsp. oil and let it get hot. Add garlic and cook just until fragrant, about 30 seconds. Remove the garlic and discard.
3. Add the onion and bell pepper and cook, frequently stirring 1-2 minutes, or until they get soft. Transfer to a bowl.
4. Add the remaining oil, if it's needed, and cook the turkey, breaking it up as it cooks until it starts to brown and the liquid has evaporated.
5. Add the vegetables back to the pan and the basil and cook another minute more. Stir in the sauce until all the ingredients are mixed well. Cook, stirring 2 minutes, or until most of the sauce is absorbed.

Nutrition

Calories: 214; Total Carbs: 7g; Net Carbs: 6g; Protein: 23g; Fat: 11g; Sugar: 5g; Fiber: 1g.

CREAMY JALAPENO CORN

5
Minutes

15
Minutes

2

Ingredients

- 1 cup corn kernels, fresh
- ¼ cup Red bell pepper, diced
- 1 Jalapeno, seeded and diced
- 1.5 ounces Cream cheese
- 1 tbsp. Olive oil
- ¼ tsp. Black pepper, ground
- ¼ cup Cheddar cheese, low-sodium

Directions

1. Preheat your oven to 350°F.
2. In a medium saucepan, sauté the bell pepper and jalapeno in the olive oil until softened, about four minutes. Add the cream cheese and continue to stir until it melts and combines with the vegetables.
3. Add in the corn, black pepper, and half of the cheese. After the mixture is combined, sprinkle the remaining cheese over the top and place the saucepan in the oven to cook until it is hot and bubbling for about fifteen minutes.

Nutrition

Calories: 284; Protein: 7g; Phosphorus: 200mg; Potassium: 293mg; Sodium: 82mg; Fat: 19g; Total Carbohydrates: 20g; Net Carbohydrates: 18g.

HAPPY HEART ENERGY BITES

20 Minutes

30 Minutes

2

Ingredients

- 1 cup rolled oats
- ¾ cup chopped walnuts
- ½ cup natural peanut butter
- ½ cup ground flaxseed
- ¼ cup honey
- ¼ cup dried cranberries

Directions

1. Combine the oats, walnuts, peanut butter, flaxseed, honey, and cranberries in a large bowl. Refrigerate for 10 to 20 minutes, if you can, to make them easier to roll.
2. Roll into ¾-inch balls. Store in the fridge or freezer if they don't disappear first.

Nutrition

Calories: 174; Total Fat: 10g; Saturated Fat: 1g; Cholesterol: 0mg; Sodium: 43mg; Carbohydrates: 17g; Fiber: 3g; Added Sugars: 7g; Protein: 5g; Potassium: 169mg; Vitamin K: 1mcg.

BLUEBERRY-RICOTTA SWIRL

5
Minutes

5
Minutes

2

Ingredients

- ½ cup fresh or frozen blueberries
- ½ cup part-skim ricotta cheese
- 1 tsp. sugar
- ½ tsp. lemon zest (optional)

Directions

1. If using frozen blueberries, warm them in a saucepan over medium heat until they are thawed but not hot.
2. Meanwhile, mix the sugar with the ricotta in a medium bowl.
3. Mix the blueberries into the ricotta, leaving a few out. Taste, and add more sugar if desired. Top with the remaining blueberries and lemon zest (if using).

Nutrition

Calories: 113; Total Fat: 5g; Saturated Fat: 3g; Cholesterol: 19mg; Sodium: 62mg; Carbohydrates: 10g; Fiber: 1g; Added Sugars: 2g; Protein: 7g; Potassium: 98mg; Vitamin K: 7mcg.

CHICKEN PEPPER BACON WRAPS

10
Minutes

15
Minutes

4

Ingredients

- 1 medium onion, chopped
- 12 strips bacon, halved
- 12 fresh Jalapeños peppers
- 12 fresh banana peppers
- 2 pounds boneless, skinless chicken breast

Directions

1. Grease a grill rack with cooking spray and preheat the grill on low heat.
2. Slice the peppers in half lengthwise, then remove their seeds.
3. Dice the chicken into small pieces and divide them into each pepper.
4. Now spread the chopped onion over the chicken in the peppers.
5. Wrap the bacon strips around the stuffed peppers.
6. Place these wrapped peppers on the grill and cook them for 15 minutes.
7. Serve fresh and warm.

Nutrition

Calories 71; Protein: 10g; Carbohydrates: 1g; Fat: 3g; Cholesterol: 26mg; Sodium: 96mg; Potassium: 147mg; Phosphorus: 84mg; Calcium: 9mg; Fiber: 0.8g.

HERBAL CREAM CHEESE TARTINES

| 15 Minutes | 15 Minutes | 2 |

Ingredients

- 1 garlic clove, halved
- 1 cup cream cheese spread
- ¼ cup chopped herbs such as chives, dill, parsley, tarragon, or thyme
- 2 tbsp. minced French shallot or onion
- ½ tsp. black pepper
- 2 tbsp. water

Directions

1. In a medium-sized bowl, combine the cream cheese, herbs, shallot, pepper, and water with a hand blender.
2. Serve the cream cheese with the rusks.

Nutrition

Calories: 476; Fat: 9g; Carbs: 75g; Protein: 23g; Sodium: 885mg; Potassium: 312mg; Phosphorus: 165mg.

Soups &
Stews

ONE-POT CHICKEN PIE STEW

15 Minutes

75 Minutes

8

Ingredients

- 1½ pounds fresh chicken breast (skinless and boneless)
- 2 cups low-sodium chicken stock
- ¼ cup canola oil
- ½ cup flour
- ½ cup fresh carrots (diced)
- ½ cup fresh onions (diced)
- ¼ cup fresh celery (diced)
- ½ tsp. black pepper
- 1 tbsp. Italian seasoning (sodium-free)
- 2 tsp. low-sodium better than bouillon® chicken base
- ½ cup frozen sweet peas (thawed)
- ½ cup heavy cream
- 1 frozen piecrust (cooked, broken into bite-sized pieces)
- 1 cup cheddar cheese (low-fat)

Directions

1. Start by pounding the chicken to tenderize it. Cut into small, equal-sized cubes.
2. Place it over a medium-high flame. Add in the stock and the chicken. Cook for about 30 minutes.
3. Add in the flour and oil. While the chicken is cooking. Mix well to combine.
4. Stir the flour and oil mixture into the broth mixture. Keep stirring until the chicken broth starts to thicken.
5. Reduce the flame to low and cook for another 15 minutes.
6. Now add carrots, celery, onions, Italian seasoning, bouillon, and black pepper. Cook for another 15 minutes.
7. Add in the cream and peas after turning off the flame. Keep stirring to mix well.
8. Transfer into soup mugs and top with the cheese and broken pie crust pieces.

Nutrition

Protein: 26g; Carbohydrates: 22g; Fat. 21g; Cholesterol: 82mg; Sodium: 424mg; Potassium: 209mg; Phosphorus: 290mg; Calcium: 88mg; Fiber: 2g.

VEGETABLE MINESTRONE

20
Minutes

20
Minutes

6

Ingredients

- 1 tsp. olive oil
- ½ sweet onion, chopped
- 1 celery stalk, diced
- 1 tsp. minced garlic
- 2 cups sodium-free chicken stock
- 1 zucchini, diced
- ½ cup shredded stemmed kale
- Freshly ground black pepper
- 1-ounce grated Parmesan cheese

Directions

1. Prepare a large saucepan over medium-high heat.
2. Add the onion, celery, and garlic. Sauté until softened, about 5 minutes.
3. Stir in the stock, zucchini, and bring to a boil. Let it simmer for 15 minutes.
4. Stir in the kale and season with pepper.
5. Garnish with the parmesan cheese and serve.

Nutrition

Calories: 100; Fat: 3g; Carbohydrates: 6g; Protein: 4g; Sodium: 195mg; Phosphorus: 70mg; Potassium: 200mg.

MEXICAN-STYLE CHICKEN AND VEGETABLE SOUP

40
Minutes

120
Minutes

4

Ingredients

- 1 soup chicken
- 3 onions
- 2 carrots
- 150 g celery root
- 1 bay leaf
- 2 cloves
- 1 tsp. peppercorns
- 1 tbsp. rapeseed oil
- 2 green peppers
- 1 red chili pepper
- 6 Red bell peppers
- 1 can kidney beans
- 1 can corn
- Salt - pepper

Directions

1. Wash the chicken soup and cover it with cold water in a large saucepan. Simmer. Boil. Meanwhile, peel 2 onions, carrots, and celery, and roughly dice them.
2. Add the bay leaves, cloves, and peppercorns to the chicken and cook for about 2 hours over medium heat. If necessary, skim off the foam occasionally and add water.
3. Take the chicken out of the soup. Strain the stock and measure 1 liter (otherwise, use the remainder). Peel the chicken, and the skin is removed. Have the meat cut into some strips.
4. Peel the remaining onion and dice it. In a saucepan, sweat in hot oil until it is translucent. Pour the stock into it and bring it to a boil. In the meantime, wash, cut in half, clean and dice the peppers and chili. Scald the hot-water Red bell peppers, rinse, peel, quarter, core, and dice. Drain the beans and maize and add bell pepper, chili, Red bell peppers, and chicken to the soup.
5. For about 15 minutes, let everything simmer together. Season with pepper and salt, and serve.

Nutrition

Calories/Energy: 69 Kcal; protein: 5.13g; Carbs: 7.87g; Lipids: 2.01g; Sodium: 347mg; Calcium: 11mg; Potassium: 153mg; Phosphorous: 44mg.

TASTY PUMPKIN SOUP

| 10 Minutes | 30 Minutes | 6 |

Ingredients

- 2 cups pumpkin puree
- 1 cup coconut cream
- 4 cups vegetable broth
- 1/2 tsp. ground ginger
- 1 tsp. curry powder
- 2 shallots, chopped
- 1/2 onion, chopped
- 4 tbsp. butter
- Pepper
- Salt

Directions

1. Melt butter in a saucepan over medium heat.
2. Add shallots and onion and sauté until softened.
3. Add ginger and curry powder and stir well.
4. Add broth, pumpkin puree, and coconut cream and stir well. Simmer for 10 minutes.
5. Puree the soup using an immersion blender until smooth.
6. Season with pepper and salt.
7. Serve and enjoy.

Nutrition

Calories: 229; Fat: 18.4g; Carbohydrates: 13g; Sugar: 4.9g; Protein: 5.6g; Cholesterol: 20mg; Phosphorus: 120mg; Potassium: 137mg; Sodium: 95mg.

DELICIOUS TOMATO BASIL SOUP

10
Minutes

20
Minutes

6

Ingredients

- 28 oz. can tomato, diced
- 1 1/2 cups chicken stock
- 1/2 tsp. Italian seasoning
- 1/2 tsp. garlic, minced
- 1 onion, chopped
- 1/4 cup fresh basil leaves
- 1/2 cup heavy cream
- 2 tbsp. butter
- Pepper
- Salt

Directions

1. Melt butter in a saucepan over medium-high heat.
2. Add onion and garlic sauté for 5 minutes.
3. Add red bell peppers, Italian seasoning, and broth. Stir well and bring to boil over high heat.
4. Turn heat to medium-low and simmer for 8–10 minutes.
5. Blend the soup using an immersion blender until smooth.
6. Add heavy cream and basil and stir well. Season soup with pepper and salt.
7. Stir and serve.

Nutrition

Calories: 108; Fat: 7.8g; Carbohydrates: 9.1g; Sugar: 5.5g; Protein: 1.9g; Cholesterol: 24mg; Phosphorus: 110mg; Potassium: 137mg; Sodium: 95mg.

JAPANESE ONION SOUP

| 15 Minutes | 45 Minutes | 4 |

Ingredients

- ½ stalk celery, diced
- 1 small onion, diced
- ½ carrot, diced
- 1 tsp. fresh ginger root, grated
- ¼ tsp. fresh garlic, minced
- 2 tbsp. chicken stock
- 3 tsp. beef bouillon granules
- 1 cup fresh shiitake, mushrooms
- 2 qrts. water
- 1 cup baby Portobello mushrooms, sliced
- 1 tbsp. fresh chives

Directions

1. Take a saucepan and place it over high heat, add water, bring to a boil.
2. Add beef bouillon, celery, onion, chicken stock, and carrots, half of the mushrooms, ginger, and garlic.
3. Put on the lid and reduce heat to medium, cook for 45 minutes.
4. Take another saucepan and add another half of the mushrooms.
5. Once the soup is cooked, strain the soup into the pot with uncooked mushrooms.
6. Garnish with chives and enjoy!

Nutrition

Calories: 25; Fat: 0.2g; Carbohydrates: 5g; Protein: 1.4g; Phosphorus: 210mg; Potassium: 217mg; Sodium: 75mg.

AMAZING ZUCCHINI SOUP

10
Minutes

20
Minutes

4

Ingredients

- 1 onion, chopped
- 3 zucchinis, cut into medium chunks
- 2 tbsp. coconut almond milk
- 2 garlic cloves, minced
- 4 cups chicken stock
- 2 tbsp. coconut oil
- Pinch salt
- Black pepper to taste

Directions

1. Take a pot and place it over medium heat.
2. Add oil and let it heat up.
3. Add zucchini, garlic, onion, and stir.
4. Cook for 5 minutes.
5. Add stock, salt, pepper, and stir.
6. Bring to a boil and reduce the heat.
7. Simmer for 20 minutes.
8. Remove from heat and add coconut almond milk.
9. Use an immersion blender until smooth.
10. Ladle into soup bowls and serve.
11. Enjoy!

Nutrition

Calories: 160; Fat: 2g; Carbohydrates: 4g; Protein: 7g; Phosphorus: 110mg; Potassium: 117mg; Sodium: 75mg.

Salads

TORTELLINI SALAD

5
Minutes

10
Minutes

4

Ingredients

- 200g tortellini with meat filling
- 100g red peppers
- 1 tomato - 1 garlic clove
- Salt pepper
- fresh basil, some leaves
- 3 tbsp. rapeseed oil
- 1 tbsp. white wine vinegar

Directions

1. Cook the tortellini in salted water according to the instructions on the packet and drain.
2. Finely dice the pepper and garlic and sweat in the rapeseed oil. Add the vinegar and spices and pour over the tortellini. Cut the tomato into small pieces and mix in. mix with the fresh basil and season to taste.

Nutrition

Energy: 161g; Protein: 4g; Fat: 9g; Carbohydrates: 18g; Dietary Fibers: 3g; Potassium: 173mg; Phosphate: 80mg Sodium 127mg

EGG TUNA SALAD

| 10 Minutes | 5 Minutes | 6 |

Ingredients

- 8 eggs, hard-boiled, peeled and chopped
- 1/8 tsp. paprika
- 1 tsp. Dijon mustard
- 2 tbsp. mayonnaise
- 1/3 cup yogurt
- 2 tbsp. chives, minced
- 2 tbsp. onion, minced
- 5 oz tuna, drain
- Pepper
- Salt

Directions

1. In a large bowl, whisk together mustard, mayonnaise, yogurt, pepper, and salt.
2. Add eggs, chives, onion, and tuna and mix well.
3. Sprinkle with paprika and serve.

Nutrition

Calories: 159; Fat: 9.6g; Carbohydrates: 3g; Sugar: 1.9g; Protein: 14.6g; Cholesterol: 228mg; Phosphorus: 110mg; Potassium: 117mg; Sodium: 75mg

PROTEIN-PACKED SHRIMP SALAD

10 Minutes	10 Minutes	4

Ingredients

- 1 lb. shrimp, peeled and deveined
- 1 ½ tbsp. fresh dill, chopped
- 1 tsp. Dijon mustard
- 2 tsp. fresh lemon juice
- 2 tbsp. onion, minced
- ½ cup celery, diced
- ½ cup mayonnaise
- Pepper
- Salt

Directions

1. Add shrimp in boiling water and cook for 2 minutes. Drain well and transfer to a large bowl.
2. Add remaining ingredients into the bowl and mix well.
3. Serve and enjoy.

Nutrition

Calories: 258; Fat: 11.9g; Carbohydrates: 10.4g; Sugar: 2.3g; Protein: 26.5g; Cholesterol: 246mg; Phosphorus: 135mg; Potassium: 154mg; Sodium: 75mg

PUMPKIN AND WALNUT PUREE

10 Minutes   10 Minutes   6

Ingredients

- 100 g walnuts, without shell
- 300 g pumpkin
- 30 ml of almond milk
- 600 ml of water

Directions

1. Peel the walnuts and pound them with the mortar.
2. Peel the pumpkin and cut it into pieces. Place the pumpkin pieces in a plastic bag and place them in the microwave over a high temperature for five minutes.
3. Put the water with the pumpkin and walnuts in the blender and puree.
4. Put everything in a saucepan and cook until mushy over low heat.
5. Slowly pour in the almond milk and stir.

Nutrition

Calories: 53, Carbohydrates: 4g; Fat: 4g; Cholesterol: 1mg; Sodium: 167mg; Potassium: 201mg; Calcium: 23mg; Phosphorus: 59mg; Dietary Fiber: 1.2 g

PESTO PASTA SALAD

| 15 Minutes | 15 Minutes | 4 |

Ingredients

- 1 cup fresh basil leaves
- ½ cup packed fresh flat-leaf parsley leaves
- ½ cup arugula, chopped
- 2 tbsp. Parmesan cheese, grated
- ¼ cup extra-virgin olive oil
- 3 tbsp. mayonnaise - 2 tbsp. water
- 12 ounces whole-wheat rotini pasta
- 1 red bell pepper, chopped
- 1 medium yellow summer squash, sliced
- 1 cup frozen baby peas

Directions

1. Boil water in a large pot.
2. Meanwhile, combine the basil, parsley, arugula, cheese, and olive oil in a blender or food processor. Process until the herbs are finely chopped. Add the mayonnaise and water, then process again. Set aside.
3. Prepare the pasta to the pot of boiling water; cook according to package directions, about 8 to 9 minutes. Drain well, reserving ¼ cup of the cooking liquid.
4. Combine the pesto, pasta, bell pepper, squash, and peas in a large bowl and toss gently, adding enough reserved pasta cooking liquid to make a sauce on the salad. Serve immediately or cover and chill, then serve.
5. Store covered in the refrigerator for up to 3 days.

Nutrition

Calories: 378; Fat: 24g; Carbohydrates: 35g; Protein: 9g; Sodium: 163mg; Potassium: 472mg; Phosphorus: 213mg

Vegetables

SESAME-GARLIC EDAMAME

| 10 Minutes | 10 Minutes | 4 |

Ingredients

- 1 (14-ounces) package frozen edamame in their shells
- 1 tbsp. canola or sunflower oil
- 1 tbsp. toasted sesame oil
- 3 garlic cloves, minced
- ½ tsp. kosher salt
- ¼ tsp. red pepper flakes (or more)

Directions

1. Bring a large pot of water to a boil over high heat. Add the edamame, and cook just long enough to warm them up for 2 to 3 minutes.
2. Meanwhile, heat the canola oil, sesame oil, garlic, salt, and red pepper flakes in a large skillet over medium heat for 1 to 2 minutes, then remove the pan from the heat. Drain the edamame and add them to the skillet, tossing to combine.

Nutrition

Calories: 173; Total Fat: 12g; Saturated Fat: 1g; Cholesterol: 0mg; Sodium: 246mg; Carbohydrates: 8g; Fiber: 5g; Added Sugars: 0g; Protein: 11g; Potassium: 487mg; Vitamin K: 34mcg

ROSEMARY AND WHITE BEAN DIP

10
Minutes

10
Minutes

10

Ingredients

- 1 (15-ounces) can cannellini beans, rinsed and drained
- 2 tbsp. extra-virgin olive oil
- 1 garlic clove, peeled
- 1 tsp. finely chopped fresh rosemary
- Pinch cayenne pepper
- Freshly ground black pepper
- 1 (7.5-ounces) jar marinated artichoke hearts, drained

Directions

1. Blend the beans, oil, garlic, rosemary, cayenne pepper, and black pepper in a food processor until smooth.
2. Add the artichoke hearts, and pulse until roughly chopped but not puréed.

Nutrition

Calories: 75; Total Fat: 5g; Saturated Fat: 1g; Cholesterol: 0mg; Sodium: 139mg; Carbohydrates: 6g; Fiber: 3g; Added Sugars: 0g; Protein: 2g; Potassium: 75mg; Vitamin K: 1mcg

CHICKPEA FATTEH

25
Minutes

25
Minutes

8

Ingredients

- 2 (4-inch) whole-wheat pitas
- 4 tbsp. extra-virgin olive oil, divided
- 1 (15-ounces) can no-salt-added chickpeas, rinsed and drained
- 1/3 cup pine nuts
- 1 cup plain 1% yogurt
- 2 garlic cloves, minced
- ¼ tsp. salt
- ½ cup pomegranate seeds (optional)

Directions

1. Preheat the oven to 375°F.
2. Cut the pitas into 1-inch squares (no need to separate the two halves), and toss with 2 tbsp. oil in a large bowl. Spread onto a rimmed baking sheet and bake, occasionally shaking the sheet until golden brown, about 10 minutes.
3. Meanwhile, gently warm the chickpeas and 1 tbsp. oil in a small saucepan over medium-low heat, 4 to 5 minutes.
4. Toast the pine nuts in a skillet with the remaining 1 tbsp. oil over medium heat until golden brown, 4 to 5 minutes.
5. Mix the yogurt with the garlic and salt in a small bowl.
6. Transfer the toasted pitas to a wide serving bowl. Top with the chickpeas. Drizzle with the yogurt mixture, then top with the pine nuts and pomegranate seeds (if using).

Nutrition

Calories: 198; Total Fat: 12g; Saturated Fat: 2g; Cholesterol: 2mg; Sodium: 144mg; Carbohydrates: 18g; Fiber: 3g; Added Sugars: 0g; Protein: 6g; Potassium: 236mg; Vitamin K: 9mcg

ROASTED ASPARAGUS

5
Minutes

10
Minutes

4

Ingredients

- 1 tbsp. extra virgin olive oil
- 1-pound fresh asparagus
- 1 medium lemon, zested
- ½ tsp. freshly grated nutmeg
- ½ tsp. kosher salt
- ½ tsp. black pepper

Directions

1. Preheat your oven to 500°F.
2. Put asparagus on an aluminum foil and add extra virgin olive oil.
3. Prepare asparagus in a single layer and fold the edges of the foil.
4. Cook in the oven for 5 minutes. Continue roasting until browned.
5. Add the roasted asparagus with nutmeg; salt, zest, and pepper before serving.

Nutrition

Calories: 55; Fat: 3.8g; Carbs: 4.7g; Protein: 2.5g; Sodium: 98mg; Potassium: 172mg; Phosphorus: 35mg

QUINOA TABBOULEH

15
Minutes

10
Minutes

8

Ingredients

- 1 cup quinoa - 4 tsp. lemon juice
- ¼ tsp. garlic clove, diced
- 5 tbsp. sesame oil
- 2 cucumbers, chopped
- 1/3 tsp. ground black pepper
- 1/3 cup tomatoes, chopped
- ½ ounce scallions, chopped
- ¼ tsp. fresh mint, chopped

Directions

1. Pour water into the pan. Add quinoa and boil it for 10 minutes. Then close the lid and let it rest for 5 minutes more. Meanwhile, in the mixing bowl mix up together lemon juice, diced garlic, sesame oil, cucumbers, ground black pepper, tomatoes, scallions, and fresh mint.
2. Then add cooked quinoa and carefully mix the side dish with the help of the spoon.
3. Store tabbouleh for up to 2 days in the fridge.

Nutrition

Calories: 168; Fat: 9.9g; Fiber: 2g; Carbs: 16.9g; Protein: 3.6g; Potassium: (k) 492mg; Sodium: (na)

Side Dishes

CINNAMON APPLE CHIPS

5
Minutes

120/180
Minutes

4

Ingredients

- 4 apples
- 1 tsp. ground cinnamon

Directions

1. Preheat the oven to 200°F. Line a baking sheet with parchment paper.
2. Core the apples and cut them into 1/8-inch slices.
3. In a medium bowl, toss the apple slices with the cinnamon. Spread the apples in a single layer on the prepared baking sheet.
4. Cook for 2 to 3 hours, until the apples are dry. They will still be soft while hot but will crisp once completely cooled.
5. Store in an airtight container for up to four days.
6. Cooking tip: If you don't have parchment paper, use cooking spray to prevent sticking.

Nutrition

Calories: 96; Total Fat: 0g; Saturated Fat: 0g; Cholesterol: 0mg; Carbohydrates: 26g; Fiber: 5g; Protein: 1g; Phosphorus: 0mg; Potassium: 198mg; Sodium: 2mg

BASIL ZUCCHINI SPAGHETTI

70 Minutes	10 Minutes	4

Ingredients

- 1/3 cup coconut oil, melted
- 4 zucchinis, cut with a spiralizer
- ¼ cup basil, chopped
- A pinch of sea salt
- Black pepper to taste
- ½ cup walnuts, chopped
- 2 garlic cloves, minced

Directions

1. In a bowl, mix zucchini spaghetti with salt and pepper, toss to coat, leave aside for 1 hour, drain well, and put in a bowl.
2. Heat up a pan with the oil over medium-high heat, add zucchini spaghetti and garlic, stir and cook for 5 minutes.
3. Add basil and walnuts and black pepper, stir and cook for 3 minutes more.
4. Divide between plates and serve as a side dish
5. Enjoy!

Nutrition

Calories: 287; Fat: 27,8g; Fiber: 3,3g; Carbs: 8,7g; Protein: 6,3 Phosphorus: 110mg; Potassium: 117mg; Sodium: 75mg

ROASTED RED PEPPER HUMMUS

10 Minutes

10 Minutes

28

Ingredients

- 1 red bell pepper
- 1 (15-ounces) can chickpeas, drained and rinsed
- Juice of 1 lemon
- 2 tbsp. tahini
- 2 garlic cloves
- 2 tbsp. extra-virgin olive oil

Directions

1. Change an oven rack to the highest position. Heat the broiler to high.
2. Core the pepper and cut it into three or four large pieces. Arrange them on a baking sheet, skin-side up.
3. Broil the peppers for 5 to 10 minutes, until the skins are charred.
4. Cover with plastic wrap and let them steam for 10 to 15 minutes, until cool enough to handle.
5. Peel the skin off the peppers, and place the peppers in a blender.
6. Add the chickpeas, lemon juice, tahini, garlic, and olive oil.
7. Process until smooth, adding up to 1 tbsp. water to adjust consistency as desired.
8. Substitution tip: This hummus can also be made without the red pepper if desired. To do this, simply follow Step 5. This will cut the Potassium: to 59mg per serving.

Nutrition

Total Fat: 6g; Saturated Fat: 1g; Cholesterol: 0mg; Carbohydrates: 10g; Fiber: 3g; Protein: 3g; Phosphorus: 58mg; Potassium: 91mg; Sodium: 72mg

GARLIC CAULIFLOWER RICE

| 10 Minutes | 5 Minutes | 8 |

Ingredients

- 1 medium head cauliflower
- 1 tbsp. extra-virgin olive oil
- 4 garlic cloves, minced
- Freshly ground black pepper

Directions

1. Using a sharp knife, remove the core of the cauliflower, and separate the cauliflower into florets.
2. In a food processor, pulse the florets until they are the size of rice, being careful not to over-process them to the point of becoming mushy.
3. In a large skillet over medium heat, heat the olive oil. Add the garlic, and stir until just fragrant.
4. Add the cauliflower, stirring to coat. Add 1 tbsp. water to the pan, cover, and reduce the heat to low. Steam for 7 to 10 minutes, until the cauliflower is tender. Season with pepper and serve.

Nutrition

Calories: 37; Total Fat: 2g; Saturated Fat: 0g; Cholesterol: 0mg; Carbohydrates: 4g; Fiber: 2g; Protein: 2g; Phosphorus: 35mg; Potassium: 226mg; Sodium: 22mg

CAESAR SALAD

5
Minutes

5
Minutes

4

Ingredients

- 1 head romaine lettuce
- ¼ cup mayonnaise
- 1 tbsp. lemon juice
- 4 anchovy fillets
- 1 tsp. Worcestershire sauce
- Black pepper - 5 garlic cloves
- 4 tbsp. Parmesan cheese
- 1 tsp. mustard

Directions

1. In a bowl mix all ingredients and mix well
2. Serve with dressing

Nutrition

Calories: 44; Fat: 2.1g; Sodium: 83mg; Potassium: 216mg; Carbs: 4.3g; Protein: 3.2g;
Phosphorus: 45.6mg; Calcium: 19mg; Potassium: 27mg; Sodium: 121 mg

Fish & Seafood

SARDINE FISH CAKES

10
Minutes

10
Minutes

4

Ingredients

- 11 oz. sardines, canned, drained
- 1/3 cup shallot, chopped
- 1 tsp. chili flakes
- ½ tsp. salt
- 2 tbsp. wheat flour, whole grain
- 1 egg; beaten
- 1 tbsp. chives, chopped
- 1 tsp. olive oil
- 1 tsp. butter

Directions

1. Put the butter in your skillet and dissolve it. Add shallot and cook it until translucent. After this, transfer the shallot to the mixing bowl.
2. Add sardines, chili flakes, salt, flour, egg; chives, and mix up until smooth with the fork's help. Make the medium size cakes and place them in the skillet. Add olive oil.
3. Roast the fish cakes for 3 minutes from each side over medium heat. Dry the cooked fish cakes with a paper towel if needed and transfer them to the serving plates.

Nutrition

Calories: 221; Fat: 12.2g; Fiber: 0.1g; Carbs: 5.4g; Protein: 21.3g; Phosphorus: 188.7mg; Potassium: 160.3mg; Sodium: 452.6 mg

INGREDIENTS
SALMON FILLET

| 5 Minutes | 25 Minutes | 1 |

Ingredients

- 4 oz. salmon fillet
- ½ tsp. salt
- 1 tsp. sesame oil
- ½ tsp. sage

Directions

1. Rub the fillet with salt and sage. Put the fish in the tray, then sprinkle it with sesame oil.
2. Cook the fish for 25 minutes at 365°F. Flip the fish carefully onto another side after 12 minutes of cooking. Serve.

Nutrition

Calories: 191, Fat 11.6g; Fiber: 0.1g; Carbs: 0.2g; Protein: 22g; Sodium: 70.5mg; Phosphorus: 472mg; Potassium: 636.3 mg

POACHED HALIBUT IN MANGO SAUCE

10 Minutes

10 Minutes

4

Ingredients

- 1-pound halibut
- 1/3 cup butter
- 1 rosemary sprig
- ½ tsp. ground black pepper
- 1 tsp. salt
- 1 tsp. honey
- ¼ cup mango juice
- 1 tsp. cornstarch

Directions

1. Put butter in the saucepan and melt it. Add rosemary sprig. Sprinkle the halibut with salt and ground black pepper. Put the fish in the boiling butter and poach it for 4 minutes.
2. Meanwhile, pour mango juice into the skillet. Add honey and bring the liquid to a boil. Add cornstarch and whisk until the liquid starts to be thick. Then remove it from the heat.
3. Transfer the poached halibut to the plate and cut it on 4. Place every fish serving on the serving plate and top with mango sauce.

Nutrition

Calories: 349; Fat: 29.3g; Fiber: 0.1g; Carbs: 3.2g; Protein: 17.8g; Phosphorus: 154mg; Potassium: 388.6mg; Sodium: 29.3 mg

CHILI MUSSELS

7
Minutes

10
Minutes

4

Ingredients

- 1-pound mussels
- 1 chili pepper, chopped
- 1 cup chicken stock
- ½ cup almond milk
- 1 tsp. olive oil
- 1 tsp. minced garlic
- 1 tsp. ground coriander
- ½ tsp. salt
- 1 cup fresh parsley, chopped
- 4 tbsp. lemon juice

Directions

1. Pour almond milk into the saucepan. Add chili pepper, chicken stock, olive oil, minced garlic, ground coriander, salt, and lemon juice.
2. Bring the liquid to a boil and add mussels. Boil the mussel for 4 minutes or until they will open shells. Then add chopped parsley and mix up the meal well. Remove it from the heat.

Nutrition

Calories: 136; Fat: 4.7g; Fiber: 0.6g; Carbs: 7.5gProtein 15.3g; Phosphorus: 180.8mg; Potassium: 312.5mg; Sodium: 319.6 mg

SHRIMP PAELLA

5
Minutes

10
Minutes

2

Ingredients

- 1 cup cooked white rice
- 1 chopped red onion
- 1 tsp. paprika
- 1 chopped garlic clove
- 1 tbsp. olive oil
- 6 oz. frozen cooked shrimp
- 1 deseeded and sliced chili pepper
- 1 tbsp. oregano

Directions

1. Warm-up olive oil in a large pan on medium-high heat. Add the onion and garlic and sauté for 2–3 minutes until soft. Now add the shrimp and sauté for a further 5 minutes or until hot through.
2. Now add the herbs, spices, chili, and rice with ½ cup boiling water. Stir until everything is warm, and the water has been absorbed. Plate up and serve.

Nutrition

Calories: 221; Protein: 17 g; Carbs: 31g; Fat: 8g; Sodium: 235mg; Potassium: 176mg; Phosphorus: 189 mg

TUNA AND RED PEPPER STEW

15
Minutes

240
Minutes

6

Ingredients

- 1 tbsp. olive oil
- 1 onion, chopped
- 1 garlic clove, minced
- ¼ tsp. red pepper flakes, or more to taste
- ½ cup dry white wine
- 1 (14-ounces) can diced Red bell peppers
- 1-pound baby red carrots, scrubbed
- 1 tsp. paprika
- 2 lb. tuna fillet
- 2 roasted red bell peppers, seeded and cut into strips
- 3 tbsp. chopped cilantro for garnish

Directions

1. Combine the oil, onions, garlic, red pepper flakes, wine, Red bell peppers, and carrots, in a slow cooker.
2. Cover and cook on HIGH for 2 hours.
3. Add the tuna and the roasted peppers, season with the paprika, and replace the cover.
4. Continue to cook on HIGH for another 2 hours or until the tuna is fully cooked.
5. Serve at once, topped with the cilantro.

Nutrition

Calories: 107; Total Fat: 3g; Saturated Fat: 0g; Cholesterol: 8mg; Sodium: 200mg; Total Carbohydrates: 15g; Dietary Fiber: 2g; Protein: 5g; Sugars 0g

Poultry

GRILLED MARINATED CHICKEN

35 Minutes

20 Minutes

6

Ingredients

- 2-pound chicken breast, skinless, boneless
- 2 tbsp. lemon juice
- 1 tsp. sage
- ½ tsp. ground nutmeg
- ½ tsp. dried oregano
- 1 tsp. paprika
- 1 tsp. onion powder
- 2 tbsp. olive oil
- 1 tsp. chili flakes
- 1 tsp. salt
- 1 tsp. apple cider vinegar

Directions

1. Make the marinade: whisk together apple cider vinegar, salt, chili flakes, olive oil, onion powder, paprika, dried oregano, ground nutmeg; sage, and lemon juice.
2. Then rub the chicken with marinade carefully and leave for 25 minutes to marinate.
3. Meanwhile, preheat the grill to 385°F.
4. Place the marinated chicken breast in the grill and cook it for 10 minutes from each side.
5. Cut the cooked chicken on the servings.

Nutrition

Calories: 218; Fat: 8.2g; Fiber: 0.8g; Carbs: 0.4g; Protein: 32.2 g; Calcium: 29mg; Phosphorous 116mg; Potassium: 207mg; Sodium: 121 mg

TASTY TURKEY PATTIES

10 Minutes

12 Minutes

4

Ingredients

- 14.5 lb. turkey
- 1 lb. cream cheese
- 1 large egg
- 1/8 tsp. ground sage
- ½ tsp. garlic powder
- ½ tsp. black pepper
- 1 tsp. onion powder
- 1 tsp. Italian seasoning
- 3 tbsp. olive oil

Directions

1. Set cream cheese out to soften.
2. Using a fork, mash turkey with juices in a medium bowl.
3. Add the cream cheese, egg; sage, garlic powder, black pepper, onion powder, Italian seasoning and mix well.
4. Form 4 patties.
5. Heat olive oil on low hotness, in a small skillet.
6. Fry patties for 5 to 6 minutes on each side or until crispy on the outside and heated thoroughly.

Nutrition

Calories: 270, Sodium: 204mg; Dietary Fiber: 1.1g; Total Sugars 3.5g; Protein: 13.5g; Calcium: 17mg; Potassium: 143mg; Phosphorus: 100 mg

FRUITY CHICKEN SALAD

| 10 Minutes | 5 Minutes | 3 |

Ingredients

- 4 skinless, boneless chicken breast halves—cooked and diced
- 1 stalk celery, diced
- 4 green onions, chopped
- 1 golden delicious apple—peeled, cored, and diced
- 1/3 cup seedless green grapes, halved
- 1/8 tsp. ground black pepper
- ¾ cup light mayonnaise

Directions

1. In a large container, add celery, chicken, onion, apple, grapes, pepper, and mayonnaise.
2. Mix all together. Serve!

Nutrition

Calories: 196, Sodium: 181mg; Total Carbohydrate 15.6g; Dietary Fiber: 1.2g; Total Sugars 9.1g; Protein: 13.2g; Calcium: 13mg; Iron 1mg; Potassium: 115mg; Phosphorus: 88 mg

CHICKEN & CAULIFLOWER RICE CASSEROLE

15
Minutes

75
Minutes

8/10

Ingredients

- 2 tbsp. coconut oil, divided
- 3 lb. bone-in chicken thighs and drumsticks
- Salt
- ground black pepper
- 3 carrots, peeled and sliced
- 1 onion, chopped finely
- 2 garlic cloves, chopped finely
- 2 tbsp. fresh cinnamon, chopped finely
- 2 tsp. ground cumin
- 1 tsp. ground coriander
- 12 tsp. ground cinnamon
- ½ tsp. ground turmeric
- 1 tsp. paprika
- ¼ tsp. red pepper cayenne
- 1 (28 oz.) can diced Red bell peppers with liquid
- 1 red bell pepper, thin strips
- ½ cup fresh parsley leaves, minced
- Salt, to taste
- 1 head cauliflower, grated to some rice-like consistency
- 1 lemon, sliced thinly

Directions

1. Warm oven to 375°F. In a large pan, melt 1 tbsp. coconut oil at high heat. Add chicken pieces and cook for about 3–5 minutes per side or till golden brown.
2. Transfer the chicken to a plate. In a similar pan, sauté the carrot, onion, garlic, and ginger for about 4–5 minutes on medium heat.
3. Stir in spices and remaining coconut oil. Add chicken, red bell peppers, bell pepper, parsley plus salt, and simmer for approximately 3–5 minutes.
4. In the bottom of a 13x9-inch rectangular baking dish, spread the cauliflower rice evenly. Place chicken mixture over cauliflower rice evenly and top with lemon slices.
5. With foil paper, cover the baking dish and bake for approximately 35 minutes. Uncover the baking dish and bake for about 25 minutes.

Nutrition

Calories: 412; Fat: 12g; Carbohydrates: 23g; Protein: 34g; Phosphorus: 201mg; Potassium: 289.4mg; Sodium: 507.4 mg

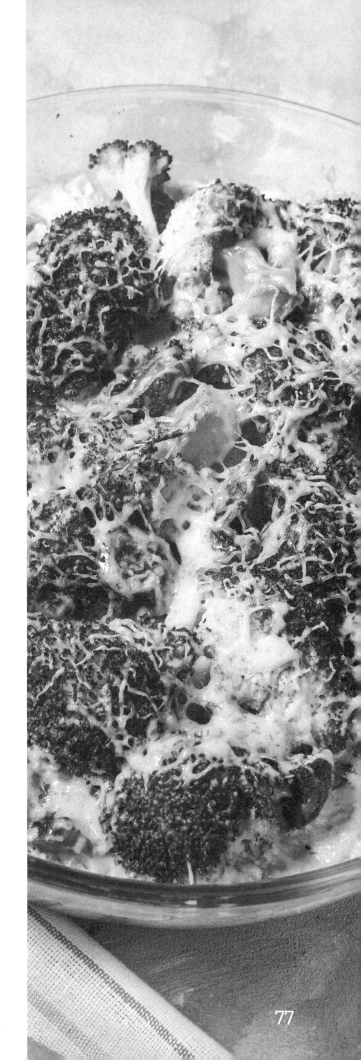

Meat

STICKY PULLED BEEF OPEN SANDWICHES

15 Minutes

300 Minutes

5

Ingredients

- ½ cup onion, sliced
- 2 garlic cloves
- 2 tbsp. fresh parsley
- 2 large carrots
- 7ounce of flat-cut beef brisket, whole
- 1 tbsp. smoked paprika
- 1 tsp. dried parsley
- 1 tsp. brown sugar
- ½ tsp. black pepper
- 2 tbsp. olive oil
- ¼ cup red wine
- 8 tbsp. cider vinegar
- 3 cups water
- 5 slices white bread
- 1 cup arugula to garnish

Directions

1. Finely chop the green onion, garlic, and fresh parsley. Grate the carrot. Put the beef in to roast in a slow cooker.
2. Add the chopped onion, garlic, and remaining ingredients, leaving the rolls, fresh parsley, and arugula to one side. Stir in the slow cooker to combine.
3. Cover and cook on low within 8 ½ to 10 hours or on high for 4 to 5 hours until tender. Remove the meat from the slow cooker. Shred the meat using two forks.
4. Return the meat to the broth to keep it warm until ready to serve. Lightly toast the bread and top with shredded beef, arugula, fresh parsley, and ½ spoon of the broth. Serve.

Nutrition

Calories: 273 Protein: 15g; Carbohydrates: 20g; Fat: 11g; Sodium: 308mg; Potassium: 399mg; Phosphorus: 159mg

PEPPERCORN PORK CHOPS

| 30 Minutes | 30 Minutes | 4 |

Ingredients

- 1 tbsp. crushed black peppercorns
- 4 pork loin chops
- 2 tbsp. olive oil
- ¼ cup butter
- 5 garlic cloves
- 1 cup green and red bell peppers
- ½ cup pineapple juice

Directions

1. Sprinkle and press peppercorns into both sides of pork chops.
2. Heat oil, butter, and garlic cloves in a large skillet over medium heat, stirring frequently.
3. Add pork chops and cook uncovered for 5–6 minutes.
4. Dice the bell peppers. Add the bell peppers and pineapple juice to the pork chops.
5. Cover and simmer for another 5–6 minutes or until pork is thoroughly cooked.

Nutrition

Calories: 317; Total Fat: 25.7g; Saturated Fat: 10.5g; Cholesterol: 66mg; Sodium: 126mg; Total Carbohydrate 9.2g; Dietary Fiber: 2g; Total Sugars 6.4g; Protein: 13.2g; Calcium: 39mg; Iron 1mg; Potassium: 250mg; Phosphorus: 115 mg

BAKED LAMB CHOPS

10
Minutes

45
Minutes

4

Ingredients

- 2 eggs
- 2 tsp. Worcestershire sauce
- 8 (5.5 oz.) lamb chops
- 2 cups graham crackers

Directions

1. Preheat the oven to 375°F.
2. In a medium bowl, combine the eggs and the Worcestershire sauce; stir well. Dip each lamb chop in the sauce and then lightly dredge in the graham crackers. Then arrange them in a 9x13-inch baking dish.
3. Bake at 375°F for 20 minutes, turn chops over, and cook for 20 more minutes, or to the desired doneness.

Nutrition

Calories176; Total Fat: 5.7g; Saturated Fat: 1.4g; Cholesterol: 72mg; Sodium: 223mg; Total Carbohydrate 21.9g; Dietary Fiber: 0.8g; Total Sugars 9.2g; Protein: 9.1g; Vitamin D 5mcg; Calcium: 17mg; Iron 2mg; Potassium: 121mg; Phosphorus: 85 mg

SHREDDED BEEF

| 10 Minutes | 300 Minutes | 4 |

Ingredients

- ½ cup onion
- 2 garlic cloves
- 2 tbsp. fresh parsley
- 2-pound beef rump roast
- 1 tbsp. Italian herb seasoning
- 1 tsp. dried parsley
- 1 bay leaf
- ½ tsp. pepper
- ¼ tsp. salt
- 2 tbsp. olive oil
- 1/3 cup vinegar
- 2 to 3 cups water
- 8 hard rolls, 3-½-inch diameter, 2 oz. each

Directions

1. Chop onion, garlic, and fresh parsley. Place beef roast in a Crock-Pot. Add chopped onion, garlic, and remaining ingredients, except fresh parsley and rolls, to Crock-Pot; stir to combine.
2. Cover and cook on low-heat setting for 8 to 10 hours, or on high setting for 4 to 5 hours, until fork-tender.
3. Remove roast from Crock-Pot.
4. Shred with two forks then return meat to cooking broth to keep warm until ready to serve.
5. Slice rolls in half and top with shredded beef, fresh parsley, and 1–2 spoons of the broth.
6. Serve open-face or as a sandwich.

Nutrition

Calories: 218; Total Fat: 9.7g; Saturated Fat: 2.6g; Cholesterol: 75mg; Sodium: 184mg; Total Carbohydrate 5.1g; Dietary Fiber: 0.4g; Total Sugars 0.4g; Protein: 26g; Calcium: 26mg; Iron 3mg; Potassium: 28mg; Phosphorus: 30mg

BEEF AND CHILI STEW

15
Minutes

420
Minutes

6

Ingredients

- ½ medium red onion sliced thinly
- ½ tbsp. vegetable oil
- 10 oz. flat-cut beef brisket, whole
- ½ cup low Sodium: stock
- ¾ cup water
- ½ tbsp. honey
- ½ tbsp. chili powder
- ½ tsp. smoked paprika
- ½ tsp. dried thyme
- 1 tsp. black pepper
- 1 tbsp. corn starch

Directions

1. Throw the sliced onion into the slow cooker first. Add a splash of oil to a large hot skillet and briefly seal the beef on all sides.
2. Remove the beef, then place it in the slow cooker. Add the stock, water, honey, and spices to the same skillet you cooked the beef meat.
3. Allow the juice to simmer until the volume is reduced by about half. Pour the juice over beef in the slow cooker. Cook on low within 7 hours.
4. Transfer the beef to your platter, shred it using two forks. Put the rest of the juice into a medium saucepan. Bring it to a simmer.
5. Whisk the cornstarch with two tbsp. water. Add to the juice and cook until slightly thickened.
6. For a thicker sauce, simmer and reduce the juice a bit more before adding cornstarch. Put the sauce on the meat and serve.

Nutrition

Calories: 128; Protein: 13g; Carbohydrates: 6g; Fat: 6g; Sodium: 228mg; Potassium: 202mg; Phosphorus: 119mg

BEEF BROCHETTES

| 20 Minutes | 60 Minutes | 1 |

Ingredients

- 1 ½ cups pineapple chunks
- 1 sliced large onion
- 2 lb. thick steak
- 1 sliced medium bell pepper
- 1 bay leaf
- ¼ cup vegetable oil
- ½ cup lemon juice
- 2 crushed garlic cloves

Directions

1. Cut beef cubes and place them in a plastic bag
2. Combine marinade ingredients in a small bowl
3. Mix and pour over beef cubes
4. Seal the bag and refrigerate for 3 to 5 hours
5. Divide ingredients onion, beef cube, green pepper, pineapple
6. Grill about 9 minutes each side

Nutrition

Calories: 304; Protein: 35g; Fat: 15 g; Carbs: 11g; Phosphorus: 264mg; Potassium: (K) 388mg; Sodium: (Na) 70 mg

Drinks & Smoothies

STRAWBERRY FRUIT SMOOTHIE

| 10 Minutes | 0 Minutes | 1 |

Ingredients

- ¾ cup fresh strawberries
- ½ cup liquid pasteurized egg whites
- ½ cup ice
- 1 tbsp. sugar

Directions

1. First, start by putting all the ingredients in a blender jug.
2. Give it a pulse for 30 seconds until blended well.
3. Serve chilled and fresh.

Nutrition

Calories: 156; Protein: 14g; Fat: 0g; Cholesterol: 0mg; Potassium: 400mg; Phosphorus: 49 mg; Calcium: 29 mg; Fiber: 2.5 g

DISTINCTIVE PINEAPPLE SMOOTHIE

5
Minutes

0
Minutes

2

Ingredients

- ¼ cup crushed ice cubes
- 2 scoops vanilla whey protein powder
- 1 cup water
- 1½ cups pineapple

Directions

1. In a high-speed blender, add all ingredients and pulse till smooth.
2. Transfer into 2 serving glasses and serve immediately.

Nutrition

Calories: 117; Fat: 2.1g; Carbs: 18.2g; Protein: 22.7g; Potassium: (K) 296mg; Sodium: (Na) 81mg; Phosphorous: 28 mg

ALMONDS & BLUEBERRIES SMOOTHIE

| 5 Minutes | 3 Minutes | 2 |

Ingredients

- ¼ cup ground almonds, unsalted
- 1 cup fresh blueberries
- Fresh juice of a 1 lemon
- 1 cup fresh kale leaf
- ½ cup coconut water
- 1 cup water
- 2 tbsp. plain yogurt (optional)

Directions

1. Dump all ingredients in your high-speed blender, and blend until your smoothie is smooth.
2. Pour the mixture into a chilled glass.
3. Serve and enjoy!

Nutrition

Calories: 110, Carbohydrates: 8g; Proteins: 2g; Fat: 7g; Fiber: 2g; Calcium: 19mg; Phosphorous 16mg; Potassium: 27mg; Sodium: 101 mg

GREEN COCONUT SMOOTHIE

10
Minutes

3
Minutes

2

Ingredients

- 1 ¼ cup coconut almond milk (canned)
- 2 tbsp. chia seeds
- 1 cup of fresh kale leaves
- 1 cup of green lettuce leaves
- 1 scoop vanilla protein powder
- 1 cup ice cubes
- Granulated stevia sweetener (to taste; optional)
- ½ cup water

Directions

1. Rinse and clean kale and the green lettuce leaves from any dirt.
2. Add all ingredients to your blender.
3. Blend until you get a nice smoothie.
4. Serve into chilled glass.

Nutrition

Calories: 179, Carbohydrates: 5g; Proteins: 4g; Fat: 18g; Fiber: 2.5g; Calcium: 22mg; Phosphorous 46mg; Potassium: 34mg; Sodium: 131 mg

CUCUMBER AND LEMON-FLAVORED WATER

| 5 Minutes | 180 Minutes | 10 |

Ingredients

- 1 lemon, deseeded, sliced
- ¼ cup fresh mint leaves, chopped
- 1 medium cucumber, sliced
- ¼ cup fresh basil leaves, chopped
- 10 cup water

Directions

1. Place the papaya and mint in a large pitcher. Pour in the water. Stir and place the pitcher in the refrigerator to infuse, overnight if possible.
2. Serve cold.

Nutrition

Calories: 10; Fat: 0g; Carbs: 2.25g; Protein: 0.12g; Sodium: 2.5mg; Potassium: 8.9mg; Phosphorus: 10mg

Desserts

GINGERBREAD LOAF

20
Minutes

60
Minutes

16

Ingredients

- Unsalted butter, for greasing the baking dish
- 3 cups all-purpose flour
- ½ tsp. baking soda substitute
- 2 tsp. ground cinnamon
- 1 tsp. ground allspice
- ¾ cup granulated sugar
- 1¼ cups plain rice almond milk
- 1 large egg
- ¼ cup olive oil
- 2 tbsp. molasses
- 2 tsp. grated fresh ginger
- Powdered sugar, for dusting

Directions

1. Preheat the oven to 350°F.
2. Lightly grease a 9-by-13-inch baking dish with butter; set aside.
3. In a large bowl, sift together the flour, baking soda substitute, cinnamon, and allspice.
4. Stir the sugar into the flour mixture.
5. In a medium bowl, whisk together the almond milk, egg; olive oil, molasses, and ginger until well blended.
6. Make a well in the center of the flour mixture and pour in the wet ingredients.
7. Mix until just combined, taking care not to overmix.
8. Pour the batter into the baking dish and bake for about 1 hour or until a wooden pick inserted in the middle comes out clean.
9. Serve warm with a dusting of powdered sugar.

Nutrition

Calories: 232; Fat: 5g; carbohydrates: 42g; phosphorus: 54mg; potassium: 104mg; sodium: 18mg; Protein: 4g

CAROB ANGEL FOOD CAKE

| 30 Minutes | 30 Minutes | 16 |

Ingredients

- ¾ cup all-purpose flour
- ¼ cup carob flour
- 1½ cups sugar, divided
- 12 large egg whites, at room temperature
- 1½ tsp. cream of tartar
- 2 tsp. vanilla

Directions

1. Preheat the oven to 375°F.
2. In a medium bowl, sift together the all-purpose flour, carob flour, and ¾ cup of sugar; set aside.
3. Beat the egg whites and cream of tartar with a hand mixer for about 5 minutes or until soft peaks form.
4. Add the remaining ¾ cup sugar by the tbsp. to the egg whites until all the sugar is used up and stiff peaks form.
5. Fold in the flour mixture and vanilla.
6. Spoon the batter into an angel food cake pan.
7. Run a knife through the batter to remove any air pockets.
8. Bake the cake for about 30 minutes or until the top springs back when pressed lightly.
9. Invert the pan onto a wire rack to cool.
10. Run a knife around the rim of the cake pan and remove the cake from the pan.

Nutrition

Calories: 113; Fat: 0g; carbohydrates: 25g; phosphorus: 11mg; potassium: 108mg; sodium: 42mg; Protein: 3g

TART APPLE GRANITA

15
Minutes

240
Minutes

4

Ingredients

- ½ cup granulated sugar
- ½ cup water
- 2 cups unsweetened apple juice
- ¼ cup freshly squeezed lemon juice

Directions

1. In a small saucepan over medium-high heat, heat the sugar and water.
2. Bring the mixture to a boil and then reduce the heat to low and simmer for about 15 minutes or until the liquid has reduced by half.
3. Remove the pan from the heat and pour the liquid into a large shallow metal pan.
4. Let the liquid cool for about 30 minutes and then stir in the apple juice and lemon juice.
5. Place the pan in the freezer.
6. After 1 hour, run a fork through the liquid to break up any ice crystals formed. Scrape down the sides as well.
7. Place the pan back in the freezer and repeat the stirring and scraping every 20 minutes, creating slush.
8. Serve when the mixture is completely frozen and looks like crushed ice, after about 3 hours.

Nutrition

Calories: 157; Fat: 0g; carbohydrates: 0g; phosphorus: 10mg; potassium: 141mg; sodium: 5mg; Protein: 0g

LEMON-LIME SHERBET

5
Minutes

15
Minutes

2

Ingredients

- 2 cups water
- 1 cup granulated sugar
- 3 tbsp. lemon zest, divided
- ½ cup freshly squeezed lemon juice
- Zest of 1 lime
- Juice of 1 lime
- ½ cup heavy (whipping) cream

Directions

1. Place a large saucepan over medium-high heat and add the water, sugar, and 2 tbsp. the lemon zest.
2. Bring the mixture to a boil and then reduce the heat and simmer for 15 minutes.
3. Transfer the mixture to a large bowl and add the remaining 1 tbsp. lemon zest, lemon juice, lime zest, and lime juice.
4. Chill the mixture in the fridge until completely cold, about 3 hours.
5. Whisk in the heavy cream and transfer the mixture to an ice cream maker.
6. Freeze according to the manufacturer's instructions.

Nutrition

Calories: 151; Fat: 6g; carbohydrates: 26g; phosphorus: 10mg; potassium: 27mg; sodium: 6mg; Protein: 0g

4 WEEK MEAL PLAN

BREAKFAST	LUNCH	DINNER	SNACK
1ST WEEK			
American Blueberry Pancakes	Beef Stir-Fry	Spicy Chili Crackers	Creamy jalapeno corn
Raspberry Peach Breakfast Smoothie	Vegetable Casserole	Spicy Cabbage Dish	Crispy parmesan cauliflower
Fast Microwave Egg Scramble	Appetizing Rice Salad	Extreme Balsamic Chicken	Cucumber dill salad with Greek yogurt dressing
Mango Lassi Smoothie	Mushrooms Velvet Soup	Enjoyable Green lettuce and Bean Medley	Zesty green beans with almonds
Breakfast Maple Sausage	Easy Lettuce Wraps	Chicken Fajitas	Cheese and Egg Breakfast Sandwich
Summer Veggie Omelet	Spaghetti with Pesto	Chicken Veronique	Peanut Butter and Banana Breakfast Sandwich
Raspberry Overnight Porridge	Corn and Shrimp Quiche	Chicken and Apple Curry	Morning Mini Cheeseburger Sliders
2ND WEEK			
Broccoli Rice Gratin (Italian Style)	Crispy Lemon Chicken	Cabbage and Beef Fry	Breakfast Muffins
Baked Curried Apple Oatmeal Cups	Mexican Steak Tacos	California Pork Chops	Tomato and Mozzarella Bruschetta
Feta Mint Omelet	Beer Pork Ribs	Caribbean Turkey Curry	All-in-One Toast
Cherry Berry Bulgur Bowl	Mexican Chorizo Sausage	Baked Macaroni & Cheese	Loaded Tater Tot Bites
Sausage Cheese Bake Omelette	Eggplant Casserole	Korean Pear Salad	Italian-Style Tomato-Parmesan Crisps
Italian Breakfast Frittata	Pizza with Chicken and Pesto	Beef Enchiladas	Baked Cheese Crisps
Mozzarella Cheese Omelette	Shrimp Quesadilla	Chicken and Broccoli Casserole	Puerto Rican Tostones
3RD WEEK			
Mexican Scrambled Eggs In Tortilla	Grilled Corn on the Cob	Pumpkin Bites	Cajun Cheese Sticks
Easy Turnip Puree	Couscous with Veggies	Feta Bean Salad	Classic Deviled Eggs
Breakfast Tacos	Easy Egg Salad	Sirloin Medallions, Green Squash, and Pineapple	Barbecue Little Smokies
Spiced French Toast	Dolmas Wrap	Seafood Casserole	Paprika Potato Chips
Chicken Egg Breakfast Muffins	Salad al Tonno	Eggplant and Red Pepper Soup	Cheddar Dip
Vegetable Tofu Scramble	Arlecchino Rice Salad	Ground Beef and Rice Soup	Coated Avocado Tacos
Keto Overnight Oats	Sauteed Chickpea and Lentil Mix	Baked Flounder	Roasted Corn with Butter and Lime
4TH WEEK			
Cheese Coconut Pancakes	Crazy Japanese Potato and Beef Croquettes	Persian Chicken	Bacon-Wrapped Onion Rings
Coconut Breakfast Smoothie	Traditional Black Bean Chili	Beef Chili	Maple Syrup Bacon
Turkey and Spinach Scramble on Melba Toast	Green Palak Paneer	Pork Meatloaf	Low-Carb Pizza Crust
Cheesy Scrambled Eggs with Fresh Herbs	Cucumber Sandwich	Chicken Stew	Colby Potato Patties
Mexican Style Burritos	Pizza Pitas	Apple & Cinnamon Spiced Honey Pork Loin	Turkey Garlic Potatoes
Bulgur, Couscous, and Buckwheat Cereal	Lettuce Wraps with Chicken	Baked Pork Chops	Creamy Scrambled Eggs
Blueberry Muffins	Turkey Pinwheels	Beef Kabobs with Pepper	Peppered Puff Pastry

Conclusion

This book is all about creating an effective renal diet, one that meets your specific needs and manages your disease. We cover the importance of protein, calories, sodium, potassium, phosphate, and fluid intake. We detail how different types of diets affect the kidney's ability to function effectively and what you should be looking for in a renal diet plan. Our kidneys are two bean-shaped organs establish on either side of our spine, just below the rib cage. One of their main functions is to filter excess fluid and waste from our blood in a process called urine formation. A healthy kidney can remove an estimated 180 liters of fluid a day!

The kidneys also help command the levels of minerals like calcium, phosphorus, and potassium in our blood. This is called electrolyte balance.

The kidneys play an even more critical role when they are diseased (called renal disease). When you have renal disease, the kidneys cannot function properly, and they begin to lose their ability to filter waste products from our blood. Since there is no longer any way for them to remove minerals like potassium, phosphate, or sodium, these minerals will build up in your blood and eventually increase fluid retention and a rise in blood pressure (hypertension). The best news is that it's possible to improve the function of your kidneys so that they can do their job as efficiently as possible. Although creatinine clearance tests are not very accurate, we can still make meaningful connections between diet and renal function. And, by following a renal diet, you can help your kidneys do what they are best at—removing waste products from your blood.

The kidneys must process four significant nutrients to do their job effectively: protein, calories, sodium, and potassium. The kidneys, like any other part of our body, need proteins to grow and function properly. Protein is essential for maintaining healthy kidney cells that can remove waste from your blood. A good rule of thumb here is that you need 0.8-1 g/kg body weight of protein each day. The better sources of protein are lean meats like chicken breast, turkey, fish, and tofu. Vegetarians can use beans and legumes to get enough protein in their diet. In this cookbook, we provide plenty of kidney-friendly protein. Be healthy and save your kidneys!

If you enjoyed this Cookbook, I would be very happy if you would support my work by leaving a positive review on Amazon.com.

For any suggestions, or if you have any complaints, before leaving a negative rating, please feel free to contact my office at terfra.innovations@gmail.com providing us with proof of purchase.

We will be happy to quickly find the best solution for you!

Caroline

Made in the USA
Las Vegas, NV
03 November 2022

58681739R00057